ADVANCE PRAISE FOR
A SPORTS ILLUSTRATED STRATEGY FOR SUCCESS
A Christian Perspective

"The emphasis to win at all cost has never been more promoted than it is in this day and age. I was told to read these scriptures as a youth after I had suffered a tough defeat—Romans 8:35-39. Reading this book gave me that same feeling as when I read those scriptures many years ago. I encourage you to read this book and put these principles into action."

—Chris Lowery, Associate Head Coach, Kansas State University

"With great reward comes great responsibility. As a professional athlete GOD has given me his GOD given talents to play sports. GOD given talents are better known as GRACE and FAVOR which GOD gives freely according to his will to whomever he please. There is nothing that we have done, or will do on our own for the talents that GOD has given us. It didn't matter how many shots I made, how many miles I ran, how many footballs I caught or how many hours I trained. GOD had already positioned me in the place I am currently, before he spoke light into the world. Life is not a game but the contrasts between the two are striking and through the spirit Christopher has revealed them.

This book is a must read!"

—Troy Hudson, NBA Veteran/Entrepreneur

A SPORTS ILLUSTRATED STRATEGY FOR SUCCESS

A Christian Perspective

WILLIAM C. HARRIS

A Sports Illustrated Strategy For Success
A Christian Perspective
© 2010 William C. Harris, Alton, Illinois

All scriptures are taken from the King James Version of the Bible, unless otherwise noted.

Commitment Prayers originally found in
Prayers that Avail Much, Volumes I and II
by Germaine Copeland

Edited and Page Design by Kate E. Stephenson
Cover Design by Javis Taylor

This book is dedicated to

my Uncle Breeze, Xenthrues Odell Cawthon,
who taught me about being a man;

my grandmother Cressie Harris,
who always had loving and encouraging words to say;

and

my grandmother "Big Willa" Cawthon, for whose selfless sacrifice,
relentless faith and fervent prayers to God on my behalf
I can never say thank you enough.

Rest in peace as you have now gone from labor to reward;
love you much!

Joshua 1:8

This book of the law shall not depart out of thy mouth; but thou shalt meditate therein day and night, that thou mayest observe to do according to all that is written therein: for then thou shalt make thy way prosperous, and then thou shalt have good success.

Table of Contents

ACKNOWLEDGMENTS

I first give thanks to the God of my salvation who makes all things possible; without Him I could do nothing; to Uncle Governor Harris, a scholar of scholars who mentors me in ministry both in scripture and life itself. Thanks for everything.

I would like to thank and acknowledge my sister (Denise Rochelle Harris-Fletcher) who taught me how to read and the importance of it.

I give honor and thanks to my parents, Rufus and Mary Harris, who nurtured and cultivated the gifts in me and inspired me to pursue every God-given opportunity.

To my loving wife Jocelyn and children, William C. Harris II ("TWO") and Ava J. Harris, for their support that empowers me, I love you with all my heart and soul; all of this is for you.

I lastly want to celebrate the "haters" who pushed me to seek the face of God for the purpose and destiny in my life. Remember, "don't hate the player, hate the game." In the end, it's all about HIM!

PREFACE

"For those whom He foreknew [of whom He was [a]aware and [b]loved beforehand], He also destined from the beginning [fore-ordaining them] to be molded into the image of His Son [and share inwardly His likeness], that He might become the firstborn among many brethren." –Romans 8:29(Amplified Bible, AMB)

Authors use the preface to amp the reader up to read further, but there is a greater significance to this preface.

It is the preface of a book that encourages us to read the entire book. Just as this book has a preface, so do our everyday lives. Every day, like sport athletes, we put on our game face before we wrestle with the cares of this world. The way in which we prepare to face life is important. Before you get out of bed, your outlook sets the tone for the day because once you leave the locker room it's on and popping. These are the moments that propel us forward into our destiny. You have to be ready to face them.

We are fashioned and shaped in inequity but He who *foreknew* us has predestined us, and being predestined, has a plan of purpose for our lives which has already been written.

This book is written to encourage you to be courageous—to look yourself in the face and begin to see who you *really* are in God. It is your destiny to prosper and be in good health even as your soul prospers. It is His will that your life be filled with success. God doesn't make any junk and everything He has made is good. So, before you face your next hurdle in life, before you swim your next lap, before you run the next play, be courageous; all of your blood, sweat and tears are but for a moment but they work for you a far more greater weight in glory.

Before you go any further in reading this book I ask that you read it in order from front to back. It is important to put

first things first, for God is orderly and we should make it a practice of becoming more like Him. *A Sports Illustrated Strategy for Success: A Christian Perspective* is written in sequence; prayerfully allow God to order your steps by reading this material in sequence. After you finish reading, you can utilize the information found in the chapters however you see fit for it to work for your present situation.

I pray that as you read this book you will gain insight and a divine connection with the purpose already within you. I declare and decree that you will not be the same. You will move forward into your destiny and achieve success with a spirit of excellence.

Tell the enemy... In Your Face!

SERENITY PRAYER

God, grant me
the serenity to accept the things I cannot change,
the courage to change the things I can,
and the wisdom to know the difference.
Amen.

~Reinhold Niebuhr

INTRODUCTION

A Sports Illustrated Strategy for Success

"This book of the law shall not depart out of thy mouth; but thou shalt meditate therein day and night, that thou mayest observe to do according to all that is written therein: for then thou shalt make thy way prosperous, and then thou shalt have good success."
— Joshua 1:8

So you've tried everything else, why not try God?

Although my background is in mechanical engineering, it doesn't take a rocket scientist to realize that there is someone greater and wiser than you or I who is able to manage the universe on a daily basis. Think about it. We never have to worry or fret over how to keep the sun shining or the moon lit. We aren't responsible for the earth's continuous rotation. But God is. Therefore, we should put our lives in the hands of the One who brings stability to everything He touches.

Whatever God does from the stars to the moon is perfect and complete. Therefore, you and I, who are his greatest creation, are perfect and complete. When you think about it, God has already taken out all the guess work about the success of life; we just have to read and follow His playbook (the B.I.B.L.E.).

God very much wants to be revealed in your life and as you begin to acknowledge Him in all of your ways He will direct your path. That's simple right? You may not see it or understand all the things you have to face; but, God has a plan for your life. It's so important for us all to walk by faith and not by sight. "Now faith is the substance of things hoped for, the evidence of things not seen" (Hebrews 11:1). Although for many of us it appears that it's a never-ending, losing battle, but the devil

1

is a liar! We are the victors and not the victim, in the end we win!

As a result of the Almighty God who is the incredible Creator that He is, we are made in His image and likeness. Therefore, no matter how bad things look, God has enabled us and empowered us with dominion to turn nothing into something. That's a God-given ability. Each and every one of us has the ability to prosper in allowing God to direct our success.

We must learn to live successful, stable, well-balanced lives by pulling from the God in us through faith. You can't see how things are going to turn out or how the situation can turn around, but the devil knows that God favors faith. That's why he tries to get you to become inconsistent in your *planning, practice and purpose.*

Scripture tells us it's IMPOSSIBLE to please God without faith and we know that He has dealt to every man a measure (portion) of faith (Romans 12:3). We have to learn how to use it to work for us. Everything starts with faith in God's word. Isn't it good to know that faith is as powerful as it is when we put it into action? Just image all the mountains that can be cast into the sea and all the water we can walk on just by applying God's Word to our everyday lives.

So who wants to be successful?

I guess that's everyone, right? Of course.

And God wants you to be successful as well.

In the opening scripture, we read from the book of Joshua. Joshua was one of the few who survived the wilderness experience. When we go through wilderness experiences (i.e. divorce, bankruptcy, death, etc.), sometimes we come out with valuable lessons but are so discouraged that we function haphazardly. Labeled unproductive persons, we can fear moving forward into the place of promise. Only when we learn to speak over our lives, meditate constantly on His word and do good, can our way be made prosperous. Only then can we have good success!

You cannot quit, stop, hesitate, or give up on what God has promised you for your life. You have to rehearse the Word of God and apply basic biblical principles—principles used by many successful individuals who have had bigger issues and worse problems than you.

Yes, that's right. If you would quit your pity party, stop telling your sad sob story and begin to look around, you might find that someone else is more disadvantaged and less fortunate than you.

Whatever your vocation or station in life, success is a perspective and not a destination. Once you reach a place of success (destiny) you have to maintain it; and sometimes maintaining a thing is more work than gaining it.

Remember, success gained can be success lost.

BEING A GOOD SPORT

And said, Naked came I out of my mother's womb, and naked
shall I return thither: the Lord gave, and the Lord hath taken
away; blessed be the name of the Lord. — Job 1:21

With a title like *A Sports Illustrated Strategy for Success: A Christian Perspective*, you would expect to hear of all the fame and fortune surrounding my talent as an A-list athlete, who lives a lavish life without boundaries: MVPs, product endorsements, pro game highlights, first class travel around the world. You probably thought you'd hear a story of a legendary pro athlete who played with some of the world's best athletes and wants to be transparent about life off the court or field. This would be great but not my calling.

I've done none of these things. Not to say that I don't have an appreciation for sports or any skills on the field, but the most that I've accomplished as an athlete is like many of you who are reading this book—I've played enough to learn how to be a good sport, in that you win some and you lose some but most importantly I was in the game.

Being a good sport means having the right spirit against adversity, accepting the challenge to finish strong. It's the conscience decision to conduct yourself with integrity and display good manners regardless of life's outcome, of whether you win or lose.

This book is not written for the purpose of obtaining material things in life. If money, cars and clothes make you, then those who made the money, cars and clothes have made you. Who does God, the Creator of all things, say that you are? The bible states that a man's worth is not based upon the consumption of his possessions (Luke 12:15), but rather the things of

God. Material things in life can become, if not careful, a distraction to the true purpose of God in your life.

The bible tells a real life story—not just a parable or some make believe story, but a true account—about a man named Job from the land of Uz who had seven sons, three daughters, seven thousand sheep, three thousand camel, five hundred yoke of oxen, five hundred she asses, and a very great household, and was considered the greatest of all the men of the east.

Sounds successful, right?

Nevertheless, the enemy *was allowed* not only to steal, kill and destroy everything within his possession, but the enemy was allowed to test and try Job's faith in God.

The enemy doesn't care about you or your stuff. His goal and purpose is to separate you from God and His will for your life. That's why the enemy comes—to test and try your patience in fulfilling God's purpose for your life on an everyday basis if you let him. But you have to take dominion and authority over every situation that arises in your life and maintain a level of integrity that stands the test of time and say, as Job did, "the Lord gave, and the Lord hath taken away; blessed be the name of the Lord" (Job 1:21).

Job maintained his faith in God and walked with integrity through sickness and disease and his foolish wife's advice to curse God and die. Job was granted double for his trouble. Everything destroyed was restored.

Yes, that's right, everything that Job had before the catastrophic events, God blessed him with double.

The question is... *Can God trust you?*

Can God trust you in the face of an enemy attack? Can He count on you to give Him the glory in the darkest hour of your life?

God needs to know that He can trust you not only with the blessings but with your relationship. Can God call you friend?

Abraham developed such a relationship with God that God called Abraham his friend (James 2:23). This is some level of commitment. That is what God requires of a friend, but there is such a huge return. If you commit yourself and your ways to Him, then you can commit yourself to the promise of purpose in your life.

Luke 18:18-34 speaks of a rich young ruler who had many possessions and in our time would be considered very successful. The rich young ruler stopped Jesus one day as He was passing by and asked the good master a question.

"What must I do to inherit the kingdom of God and eternal life?"

Jesus answered with confidence concerning keeping the law, and the rich young ruler answered proudly that he had kept the law from his childhood up. This is mistake number one in thinking that you're already in good. Secondly, for those of us who are believers, we should realize that we are the redeemed of God but we have a responsibility with purpose.

Jesus then replied to the young man, since the law is in place all you have to do is sell all that you own, give to the poor and follow me.

The rich young ruler walked away sorrowful for it was a hard thing for him to do.

Well, guess what? The story doesn't stop there. Jesus requested that He follow Him as a disciple. Jesus had purpose and need of the rich young ruler as a disciple (follower) of Him. See, above everything else God wants you and I to be on His team. He wants as many as will to come and join His franchise so we can win together forever. In life, we have to be committed to God through obedience and sacrifice.

The bible teaches us to "seek ye first the kingdom of God and His righteousness and all these other things will be added to you" (Matthew 3:33). If you want to be successful, a winner in life, first place is always with God; look to Him for direction and He shall direct you in the way that you should go. What we sometimes have to give up to really become successful in this life may cost us a hard thing but it is well worth the expense if you put things in the right perspective. God has need of each and every one of us as free agents of change to affect those around us.

There is a level of integrity, a spirit of excellence that God requires from you, even when you are faced with distractions, disappointments, destruction and even death. He requires that you remain in character with who He made you to be; we call it being a "good sport". In the end, you will come out with double for your trouble

.

PRESSING FORWARD

"Brethren, I count not myself to have apprehended: but this one thing I do, forgetting those things which are behind, and reaching forth unto those things which are before, I press toward the mark for the prize of the high calling of God in Christ Jesus."
(Philippians: 3:13)

The scripture above simply means that in our daily testament to others, we may not have already obtained success, but we know that whatever success is for us must be attained by putting all failed attempts behind us and pressing forward to the goal of high places and new faces.

In sports there is a defensive tactic called the full court press, a strategy that pressures the opposing team to travel the entire length of the court. It takes a great deal of effort and is often used when teams are behind late in the game and look to create a winning turnover. Arkansas's coach Nolan Richardson called his version of full court pressure "40 minutes of Hell". Whether it's 40 minutes or 40 years, we've all been through hell and high water, behind the half court of life and short on time. The devil is real and is always trying to press you backwards, to tire you out and force you to his side. Turn the tables.

If you are looking to start a new and successful life worth living, you first have to acknowledge the change factor. The change factor is this: if you want something that you've never had before, then you have to do something different from what you've always done. Albert Einstein once defined insanity as doing the same thing over and over again expecting a different result. My grandmother, Willa Cawthon, told me that when you ask God in prayer to fix something in your life, in answer to your prayer He may not change the situation or the environment that you're in, but He very well may change *you*. It's a tried and true lesson that it's usually "Self" that is the first thing that needs to change; not the situation, not the environment but you.

William Shakespeare said, "This above all, to thine own self be true."

Consider yourself a free agent moving in the Spirit of God, for in Him do we live, move and have our being. Stop living a life broke, busted and disgusted. Get ready to change! Remember, your attitude determines your altitude... so keep it positive. Let's move forward.

So many people, too often we sit out of the game. They'd rather do fantasy sports instead of play the game for real.

Why redshirt yourself, daydreaming all day about making life moves instead of moving?

Turn fantasy into fruition and shake that bad habit. Get up and get out!

Contrary to popular belief, life is a sport and you're made to play it one way or another. The only difference is that you have real-life wins and losses that can affect you for the rest of your life. Sitting on the bench, watching others move the ball up and down the court doesn't get *you* very far, just life full of regrets.

When you talk about a life of regrets, three individuals come to mind; their names are **Should've**, **Could've** and **Would've**.

In reality championships are played and won by everyday people whose hard work, talents and skills pay off for them. But they are the ones who are driven to play. You have to make the conscious decision to play.

As 21st century post-modern believers, we have to learn to play hard or go home, and we all know, going home ain't no fun. Don't be a loser. Live life on purpose and die empty in knowing you gave it your all to live a full life.

Matthew 25:14-28 tells a story about a master who gave one servant five talents, another servant two, and the last servant one talent. All invested their talents and produced a greater return on investment except the servant with one talent who decided to bury it in the earth. The master returned looking to see growth, productivity, wins and advancements from everyone but found only two faithful. The one who failed to get in the game of life was punished for poor performance and lack of participation. He was cast into outer darkness.

Sometimes our dark and grim experiences are the results of burying our heads in the sand with our hands in our pocket. God has given us all talents, gifts, skills and abilities to us productively here *on* earth, but too many of us are burying our heads *in* the earth not producing anything. What a waste.

You are worth more than a buried talent; you are more than a hidden treasure. You are responsible for believing in yourself, knowing you are valuable and worthy of multiplying your talent. With a God-given strategy, your life will reap success!

You've got to learn how *not* to get hung up on your hang ups. Letting others determine your level of success is a trap. A trick of the enemy is to hold you in bondage, to prevent you from having dominion in every area of your life.

Think about it this way, and be honest. Why would you allow anyone other than God, the author and finisher of our faith, have more to say about your life than He who created you for His glory?

It's hard enough for you to determine what you deem success; how can anyone else determine it for you other than God Himself? Speak over yourself and encourage yourself in the Lord. All of the other voices are a distraction. Don't drop the ball. You've got to work what's been given to you.

Listen, even Jesus had haters who could have deterred Him from the Father's mandate. Without his sacrifice on the cross there would be no redemption for our sins! But, for the joy that was set before Him, He endured the hardship and became the firstborn of God that we might be saved!

Can you imagine being separated from the greatest life coach in history, God the Father, for an eternity? Think about it, what if Jesus had been talked out of his destiny. Where would we be?

Eternal damnation.

Praise be to God for His son, Jesus Christ who has given us the victory in every area in our lives! Be assured that God will bring you into a place of promise, your expected end to a new beginning. You have to know God has an expected (blessed) place called destiny for you. Where you are today is not where he would have you to be tomorrow. The troubles you are facing are going to end and a new day with new mercies is on the horizon. God's expectation of man is far greater than any expectation of man for your life. The Bible says in 2 Corinthians 2:19, "But as it is written, Eye hath not seen, nor ear heard, neither have entered into the heart of man, the things which God hath prepared for them that love him." There is so much more to your life than where you are now, but it's according to your faith. You must press forward! Forget the disappointments of the past (i.e. the divorce, the foreclosure, the loss of a job, the cancelled promotion) and see the things of God in your future. Wine is more expensive than a bag of grapes because they've gone through a press. Your life is worth more and will produce more if you have the faith to press on. Remember, you have the whole host of heaven cheering for you!

BEING A CLUTCH SHOOTER

Stand fast therefore in the liberty wherewith Christ hath made us free, and be not entangled again with the yoke of bondage.
– Galatians 5:1

It's important how we play out the life situations that bring the most pressure. We all have our methods to handle the madness. There are times when the game is tight and we need someone who won't choke under pressure to win the game for our team. These individuals are called Clutch Shooters. One of the NBA's all time greats, an icon to the world of sports is Jerry West, better known as "The Clutch". The logo used to brand the NBA league uses his silhouette—this is huge. It shows just how important it is to be reliable under pressure.

Can you handle pressure? Are you able to win one for team "self" without chocking on opportunity? Can God count on you to be the next "poster-child" to brand his kingdom and make his name glorious?

In the Old Testament, there's a story of three Hebrew boys named Shadrach, Meschach and Ebednego who trusted God with their lives (Daniel 1-3). They were at the top their game and were the king's choice men (His Starters, you could say). To make a long story short, their faith was challenged and their lives were on the line. They failed to bow and worship an idol set by the king and were sentenced to a fiery furnace, one heated seven times hotter than normal. They did not waiver in their faith and allegiance to the God of Israel. As a result, God Himself entered the furnace with them. The very men that threw them in were the ones burned to death. The bible says that when Shadrach, Meschach and Ebednego walked out of the furnace there was no heat or smell, neither was one hair on their heads burned. After their release they were promoted above all the magistrates in the kingdom. To be selected for the Heisman or as MVP, you have to handle pressure. And sometimes, it's turned up seven times hotter than that on the average player. *What do you do when your promotion is under fire?*

Sports can be enjoyable but playing isn't always fun. Like sports, life has its misfortunes and mishaps that make you want to quit, give up and throw in the towel. You have to be determine to go another round. If everyone threw in the towel, who would be left standing?

God is saying to you today, right now, "Stand fast (still and rooted) therefore in the liberty wherewith Christ has set you free, and be not entangled again with the yoke of bondage (as a result of all you've been through in life)." This simply means that you are now liberated from your past mistakes, failures, hurts and pains and are free to live, love and laugh, knowing that Christ has set you free to experience a new life in Him that is whole and complete; a life of success. God's word illustrates life as a sport in which we all play. The thing that we must understand is that the game is already fixed. We just have to tap in and listen to the instructions of God and do things His way. He's the greatest life coach of all times. Whatever you need to learn how to be successful... it's in the playbook, the Good Book called the BIBLE.

PART 1: PLANNING – TRAINING

"Go, consecrate the people. Tell them, 'Consecrate yourselves in preparation for tomorrow; for this is what the LORD, the God of Israel, says: There are devoted things among you, Israel. You cannot stand against your enemies until you remove them."
–Joshua 7:13

It's a known fact that athletes need to practice and regularly train in order to perform well. Training efficiently with routine workouts and skill drills can help you avoid injuries, burnout and boredom, as well as reach new levels of performance.

It is so important to understand early on in life that most of the work put in to becoming successful is not done on the spot, it's not something produced during the game but much of what it takes to be successful is developed before the game in training. This is the reason why so much more attention is given to the training section of this book than the actual strategies section. Thomas Edison said, "Success is 90% perspiration, 10% inspiration". What a person produces during the game only reflects the work put in during practice. What you want to achieve on the court, in the boardroom or classroom, you should have already prepared yourself for before walking through the door. Everyone wants an opportunity to compete but few want to prepare for it.

Once an athlete reaches a certain level of performance, corporate America endorses him or her to market a given product or brand. Usually this level of achievement occurs after a certain level of commitment to the game is reached. Much like corporate America, those of us who are kingdom-minded understand that God endorses or favors his own. Those who are given to a certain level of commitment, produce a certain level of favor! God's brand is so BIG (Psalm 24:1-5) that he entrust the gifts, talents and abilities to YOU to perform and carry out his purpose he has for your life. But there is a certain level that only *you* can produce; you have to be committed in doing so and he rewards you with greatness.

Real men and women train, they prepare for the worst and practice to be ready to receive the good—good works that glorify the Father.

Train your body, soul and mind to respond but not react to the negative things the enemy brings your way. Training increases your chances of success and helps to eliminate careless failures. It allows you to maneuver, bob-and-weave, through life circumstances that may be unfavorable in the moment but work for your good, to them who love God and are called according to their purpose (Romans 8:28). You have one of two choices—Go hard or go home! You either train or lose your position (heir to the kingdom) with the Father.

Think about Christ; the biggest fight of His life was dying for our sins on the cross. He didn't wait 'til they whipped and beat him, spit on him and nailed him to the cross to prepare himself. He often went away to pray, he fasted for 40 days to resist temptation, he pushed beyond self and became selfless with no strings attached for the sins of the world...that's BIG!

If you want to be successful you will spend time and attention training for it.

EYE–HAND COORDINATION

"And the Lord answered me, and said, write the vision, and make it plain upon tables, that he may run that that readeth it."
— Habakkuk 2:2

Baseball requires good eye–hand coordination. To make the bat hit the ball begins long before your arm swings; it starts with the eye. Whether up at bat or catching balls in the outfield, MLB athletes need to have strong, accurate eye–hand coordination—the ability to see your goal and create positive motion to meet it. This is the first skill needed to attain golden status in the diamond and is developed through diligent practice.

Habakkuk 2:2, what an awesome and prophetic word for anyone. First and foremost this scripture actualizes the fact that the Lord really does answer prayer and the dream life that you envision can be more than a fantasy but fruition (it bears fruit).

When you are a dreamer and have a vision for your life to be more than what it is right now you have to write it down and make it plain.

K.I.S.S. is a popular acronym in business that stands for Keep It Simple Stupid. Go ahead and blow yourself a kiss. This scripture tells us to keep it simple, to make your vision clear so that others who've got your back can better assist you as you cast your vision.

Forrest Gump is a popular movie, released in 1994. As naïve and slow-witted as he was, Forrest Gump had dreams and aspirations (vision); many of which included others and their desires. Forrest had the ability to "see it before it was in his hands." That's the power of vision. One day Forrest felt the urge to run and so he did. Forrest kept running and running until others, without rhyme or reason, joined him. Isn't amazing how the thing that drives you can drive others? Forrest's vision eventually influenced all of American culture. Vision is that powerful in that it takes the form of a runner who builds momentum and influences others, sometime a whole nation to respond to what started out as a slow jog of an idea.

Helen Keller, a renowned blind and partially deaf American activist, once stated "Character cannot be developed in ease and quiet. Only through experience of trial and suffering can the soul be strengthened, ambition inspired, and success achieved". She also stated that "The only thing worse than being blind is having sight but no vision".

Vision is so important to everyday life that we so often take it for granted. Vision is more than having the sense of sight, of being able to physically look at things around us, but vision empowers us to create. This is the very thing God himself did. He envisioned a world therefore He created. Many of us as Christian believers have sight—the ability to look with the natural eye—but few of us have faith in our *vision*, the ability to see ourselves functioning and operating in a much larger capacity, at a greater level than we are right now.

Every celebrated athlete of any sport has good eye–hand coordination and as believers, so should we.

We have to know without a shadow of doubt that we can hit homeruns because our hearts make contact with God through obedience to His word. It's all about relationship. God has good eye–hand coordination, He knows where He wants you to be in life and He knows how to get you there. We are responsible for developing this same skill, eye–hand coordination (vision to action), to *see* who we are to *become* in God. Eye–hand coordination starts with prayer, consecration and reading His Word—conferring with God to see where He wants us in life. This has to happen before—before we receive the job promotion, before we grasp the gold, before we can grab the ring. We have to *see* it ahead of time and plan for it.

All too often we allow our past and present problems to block the blessings of God for our future. Takes some time to envision the person God created you to be. Vision is more than seeing yourself driving a new car, living in a new home, or starting a new ministry. Vision is responsible for prophetic manifestation in real-time, meaning that everything begins with an idea.

Vision is defined in Webster's Dictionary as:

1

a : something seen in a dream, trance, or ecstasy; *especially* : a supernatural appearance that conveys a revelation

b : a thought, concept, or object formed by the imagination

c : a manifestation to the senses of something immaterial <look, not at *visions,* but at realities — Edith Wharton>

2

a : the act or power of imagination

b (1) : mode of seeing or conceiving *(2)* : unusual discernment or foresight <a person of *vision*>

c : direct mystical awareness of the supernatural usually in visible form

Let me give you biblical basis for this concept. Uncle Governor, one of the most influential men in my life revealed to me in Genesis 1-2 that God first created (imagined) in Chapter 1, then He made (formed) in Chapter 2. This passage of scripture is so impactful concerning vision; God first had a vision of what the world could be. He imagined and then manifested something out of nothing. Vision is powerful. It is a direct connection with God and the larger plan, the BIG picture, He has for your life.

God is never unorganized in anything He does, including His thoughts. The late Pastor C.B. Brown (my wife's grandfather) would say, "God never gives you anything out of control, if it gets out of control you allowed it".

God in his awesome infinite wisdom revealed something else to me in defining the word vision. The word vision carries another word, "ion". An ion is the smallest part of a substance. So with vision, God is also saying to you and I, we must be able to see the Big Picture while paying attention to the *smallest* details in life. Not only being on top is significant but the little things carry value too.

A lot of times, if not careful, we become distracted in life simply because things don't add up; it's not apparent that God's hand is involved in the things we face day to day. My brother-in-law Joe Fletcher calls it ADD—Another Devilish Distraction.

You know the times when God has promised you something as simple as providing your needs everyday and then you open up a disconnect notice; that's one of those devilish distractions.

How about your marriage? You know that God put you together but you and your spouse seem to fight over the smallest thing…that's another devilish distraction.

The Devil doesn't want you to see things as they really are; he doesn't want you to have clarity about God's word concerning your life therefore he tries to distract you to bring discouragement. But Proverbs 3:4 says, "Trust in the Lord with all thine heart; and lean not unto thine own understanding." When things don't seem to add up in your life, because the devil is busy ADDing it up for you, *you* are still responsible for *trusting* God.

I had to trust God in writing this book; I've never taken a greater leap of faith. I thought to myself am I crazy, what do I know about sports and success? I had to see God and not my own deficiencies that could distract me from fulfilling destiny for my life. When you have vision and you trust that God has a greater plan for your life, the devil can ADD 'til he's blue in the face and it won't matter...as one of my members at my church would say, write that down!

Now sometimes people have another problem; because they are so distracted, they don't really see who others are in God. They don't recognize the potential or purpose of their sisters and brothers; so they mishandle you based off their own ADDictions. As a visionary, clarity is important, not only for seeing more for yourself but recognizing the God in others. Many Pro athletes have been overlooked, not seen for the players they really are, maybe because they aren't as showy or as good looking or as diverse as another player. But we are all on the team for a reason—because each one of us brings something unique and worthwhile to the table. The question to ask is *how do you see yourself and others?* Do you see the God potential?

DIET & NUTRITION

"But he answered and said, It is written,
Man shall not live by bread alone, but by every word that
proceedeth out of the mouth of God" — Matthews 4:3-5

"Let this mind be in you, which was also in Christ Jesus"
—Philippians 2:5

We all know that much of what defines a good athlete are good genes, good training and conditioning, but you have to include a sensible diet. For peak performance, optimal nutrition is essential. The nourishment needed to think clearly, make quick plays, and endure the mental and physical wear and tear of a game comes not only from what you feed your body, but from what you feed your mind. Yes, the mind. You have to be focused to play in the game and it all starts with a balanced diet.

It's funny how nowadays everybody and their mama is dieting and watching what they eat. Dieting is so popular that it has gone mainstream; even fast food restaurants like McDonald's have changed their menus to accommodate customers watching their weight. I remember when, back in the day, we weren't worried about what we ate... and we ate everything. Now, athletic, health-conscious individuals are really conscious of their intake to the exponential power. Not only do we watch what we eat but we take supplements to enhance our performance. Whether on the field or just in the gym, we want to perform at our potential. Well, that's the same approach we should have spiritually. We should want to perform at our best and do service with a spirit of excellence. In order to avoid exhaustion and weariness in our good doings, we have to eat right.

In the bible, "It is written, Man shall not live by bread alone, but by every word that proceedeth out of the mouth of God"

(Matthew 4:4). This means that as we train and develop our gifts, talents and abilities, we have to not only watch our natural intake, but our spiritual one as well. It is vital and key to proper growth and development, for this is the temple of God in which the Holy Spirit dwells. We are not only responsible for keeping it clean but for building strength so that we may be able to stand, fight and compete against the devil, our adversary.

Being gifted and talented is one thing but operating under the anointing of God is major league status; and in order to do this you have to stir up the gift that is within you. But if there's nothing there, there's nothing to stir. We often settle for just playing school or college ball. Some of us make it to the minor leagues. But very few get to the major leagues where God wants you to be. He scouted you out before the foundations of the world and if you're like me, there's nothing like it, all the perks and benefits. I've been drafted into a heavenly team with exceptional anointing.

> "But ye are a chosen generation, a royal priesthood, an holy nation, a peculiar people; that ye should shew forth the praises of him who hath called you out of darkness into his marvellous light" (1 Peter 2:9).

It is so very important as a believer to watch what you do, watch what you say, watch where you go and watch what you eat. The enemy wants to entrap you by disregarding the things that you add to your person.

He'll make you think that it's okay. Think back to Adam and Eve when they ate of the forbidden fruit. This changed the very course of not only their lives but all mankind. We have it better now; they had no one to help them watch their weight, or should I say avoid sin through indulgence, but we do. That's what Hebrews 12 explains:

"[W]e are surrounded by so great a cloud of witnesses, let us lay aside every weight, and the sin which so easily ensnares us, and let us run with endurance the race that is set before us, looking unto Jesus, the author and finisher of our faith, who for the joy that was set before Him endured the cross, despising the shame, and has sat down at the right hand of the throne of God.

A host of witnesses are cheering us to finish the race of faith. They are helping us watch our weight and encouraging us with spiritual nutrition, as it will affect our finish. But thanks be to God who published His word on the earth for our sakes in reaching our goals.

Life is a race that must be run with diligence. Who in the world would run a race or marathon with extra weights on them? You can forget about finishing the race before you even begin.

God tells us to look to Jesus who is the author and finisher of our faith—who has written our destiny and completed the journey so that we can succeed. We have been blessed to have Christ Jesus as our model for success. He proclaims to us with surety that we too can finish strong and live a life of success because He has already overcome the world. I told you that some battles and victories won are without you, you don't have to do anything but show up and let God show out through the good works that He would have us do in His name.

Now instead of us eating the fruit from the wrong tree, we can eat of the Fruit of the Spirit—love, joy, peace, longsuffering, gentleness, goodness, faith, meekness, temperance—against such there is no law. Eating this fruit provides pure wholesome energy that is lasting and clean to the spirit.

Remember, we are what we eat.

Our decision-making skills and choices can be altered by eating the wrong things. Just because you have an appetite doesn't mean you eat stuff that burns you out! It is mandatory that we watch self indulgence, it never fills you up.

STRENGTH TRAINING

No Pain, No Gain

*"Every good gift and every perfect gift is from above, and cometh
down from the Father of lights, with whom is no variableness,
neither shadow of turning." — James 1:17-*

Sports are one of the most watched and played pastimes in
America, but everyone is not cut out to be an athlete. Some of
us are engineers, chefs, pastors, business people, you name it.
The one thing that we all have in common is we are all gifted in
something. However, *we* are responsible for cultivating our gift;
sharpening our skills, talents and abilities to become all that we
can be...that's successful. We do this by strengthening our gifts.
Strength training is vital to developing a good gift, a perfect gift
(James 1:17). There's no doubt about raw talent but it's another
level when a player has taken the time to train and sharpen
their gift for the game.

A classic American saying is "No Pain, No Gain." It takes
determination to condition yourself for such a physically de-
manding activity. In any given game there will be falls, hits,
knocks and bumps, but your resistance to withstand them all
depends on your strength training before the game. You not
only need strength for physical contact but you need strength
just to endure the length of the game. The amount of time spent
on the field can be grueling all by itself so you need fortitude to
withstand the clock. Athletes around the world, from little
league to the Olympics, train hard through disciplined activity.

It takes discipline to earn that next promotion or job inter-
view.

It takes discipline to prepare for the championship game.

25

It takes discipline to train for that apprenticeship or study for that degree.

It takes discipline to heal and mend your relationships.

It takes discipline to work at that higher level of ministry.

Discipline is very much a part of a successful life. You have to train and condition yourself to perform at a level that's above average.

The bandwagon is small if not empty when it comes to training. Training separates the men from the boys and the women from the girls. If you really want to become successful in life you must train. Train your mind, body and soul to get in alignment with your vision so that you can endure hardship as you perfect your gifts, talents, and abilities.

Michael Jordan of the Chicago Bulls conditioned himself to work out and practice before the practice. He trained himself to put in overtime so by game time he was on top of his game and ready to play at the next level—a higher level.

Where do you stand?

Are you disciplined enough to train hard?

Can you be consistent in practicing the principles that will take you to the top of your game?

How do we get to the point of conditioning our conscious to outperform beyond our last failure and our last success? This strength is not of our own but of the Lord who empowers us to endure. Scripture says, "It is God that girdeth me with strength, and maketh my way perfect" (Psalm 18:32). But while the strength comes from the Lord, the action must come from us. We have to put the work in.

As a kid on the playground, you learn early the number one rule of thumb in the hood is that you either *go hard or go home.* The streets don't play. Who wants to team up with a quitter? Nobody! Likewise in life, nobody wants a quitter on their team. No one wishes a business partner who pulls out before they even get started. Nobody wants to play with somebody who's weak and can't take a hit on the field, Right?

If you look at major league sports, many of the best MVPs and high-profile athletes come from the School of Hard Knocks. So why is it that we who believe in God expect Him to do all the work? I mean He created everything for us to have dominion over and we won't even apply energy to do what it is in our own power to do (let alone move a mountain by faith the size of a mustard seed). The bible says, "Now unto him that is able to do exceeding abundantly above all that we ask or think, according to the power that *worketh in us*" (Ephesians 3:20). Powerful scripture is often quickly read over or skipped because it isn't pretty. Genesis 3:19 says that because of man's disobedience, we were commanded to work by the sweat of our brow. It's time to sweat!

Life is not a game to take lightly, especially with the adversary, the devil, rampant and on the loose going to and fro seeking whom he may devour. Gain or success is always associated with a struggle. Real success stories only occur out of discipline and perseverance. Scripture says in Philippians 4:13, "I can do all things through Christ which strengtheneth me"; "Not by might, nor by power, but by my spirit, saith the LORD of hosts" (Zechariah 4:6).

Train Up a Child

"Train up a child in the way that he should go: and when he is old, he will not depart from it." — Proverbs 22:6

We often neglect the importance of working with our children. Many of us feel the effects of not receiving the proper guidance, especially in the areas in which we are most gifted, as a child. We may have mentors, counselors and advisors out the box but no one can replace Godly parents as the best life coaches in the world. Parents, if they are properly involved in their children's lives, will see firsthand the talents and abilities in their children that need to be cultivated.

My sister and I were blessed to have parents who have always believed that there was greatness in us and that we have God's hand and favor on our lives. They understood that it was not enough just to see it, but they had the responsibility of working with us to develop it. Before we could make decisions and choices on our own, they understood their responsibility to lead us and guide us with purpose.

Positively speaking, think about the Michael Jacksons and the Tiger Woods of life. Where would they be if their parents hadn't seen, cultivated and nurtured their gifts at an early age?

To be ahead of the game in life the gifts, talents and abilities have to be nurtured so that we become confident in the fundamentals, and challenged to be creative in exploring the many possibilities of success. You have the ability to increase your child's ability to succeed simply by working with them at an early age. The same discipline you are practicing in your own life to strengthen yourself for all of your daily battles, you need to instill that practice in your children on a daily basis. It starts with prayer and creating a vision for themselves that carries through to seeing the God in them and in others.

Each generation carrying your family name should get better, live a life more successful than the prior; but all too often, an unnerving practice of the opposite occurs. It starts with training.

Training consists of a lot of conditioning and discipline. Many successful individuals will admit that there were times when they got off track, but because of what was instilled in them early on, they had the drive to reflect and respond accordingly. Good discipline is healthy and rewarding; it does not oppress, repress or depress. Discipline measures ability performed through routine activities. The old saying goes, *practice makes perfect.* Practice positive performance and positive reinforcement. Remember, it takes discipline to get you to your destiny!

COMPETITION

"If a wise man contendeth with a foolish man, whether he rage or laugh, there is no rest." — Proverbs 29:9

This chapter is one of the most challenging topics to discuss in life. We live in a society where everyone is competitive—in sports, in the workforce, and ministry; you name it someone is competing to be on top. Contrary to popular beliefs, competition is very real; and if not careful, you will find yourself surrendering all self-worth to obtain success and still come up with the short end of the stick, *no rest*. Whether you're a college graduate seeking an entry-level position, the next possible draft pick for a pro team, or ministry leader, there will always be something pushing you to compete. Since the beginning of time and before (eternity), there has always been competition, which can lead to unproductive behavior like hate, jealousy, spite, etc. The Devil himself is an excellent example.

In eternity, the Devil who was originally in heaven was one of the chief angels, positioned as God minister of music. He was so anointed and wonderfully created that it is said he had pipe horns built into his body and very fair to look upon. Well this was not good enough for him. He was high and lifted but not enough and he sought to be as God himself. He became jealous and conspired against God and when he was kicked out of heaven to earth he took a third of heaven's angels and still today he's running to and fro in the earth (*restless*) seeking whom he may devour. Isn't that amazing? He was exalted, anointed, called upon often but not satisfied with the position and place God had for him. This is why you should never compete against someone else's gift, talent, or ability; only walk in the anointing that God gave you. First Lady Eugenia Robinson of Zion

Temple COGIC in Murphysboro, Illinois had a saying, "If you stay in your place, you will have a place to stay." (I guess it's too late to tell the devil this.)

Never compete with others only challenge yourself!

Regardless of what sport or instrument you play, what ministry you participate in, or what business you plan, always remember who you're competing against. Yes, you are responsible for putting your best foot forward. Yes, you have to accept the challenge. But ultimately challenge is within yourself. You should always challenge the gift, talent and ability in you more than you do the persons around you. It's the anointing of God in your life that the enemy hates to see advance you to that next level, not your peers. The devil doesn't want you to produce good fruit because he failed to stay in his place.

Let me give you a personal example.

The church I currently pastor, Brown's Faith Temple COGIC, was not just handed to me, but it came with many faith challenges, including the temptation to compete. I was blessed to sit under one of the world's best scholars of the gospel who many scholars themselves with large ministries across the country confide in for his biblical teachings. My pastor, Elder Governor Harris, is unusually gifted and anointed to teach God's word. Much of my learning of the scriptures has come from him and also many humbling life lessons can be attributed to his teachings. As a member of the church, both my person and faith have been tested.. See when you have a heart (passion) for what you do, you have to be careful because the enemy wants what God has for you and will try you, as our forefathers would say, "every-witcha-way". You have to have you're A-game on, otherwise you will fail the test. You see the devil comes to kill, steal and destroy; why? Because he knows that you have an inheritance with the Lord and he has nothing coming but a Devil's hell.

From my own ministry experiences, competition is a killer in the church.

The next person is always sitting there thinking that they can do it better than you. They question your calling, they ask "how do *you* know you're chosen?" The negativity starts rolling with the comments: "You're too young." "You're not ready." "You're not good enough." "You aren't smart enough." "You won't amount to anything..."

This is where you have to be careful because if not, you will be tempted to try and prove a point that God already has covered. It takes maturity and good discipline (training) to wait for your appointed time. You have to know your capabilities, your limits and your weaknesses too. Especially weaknesses, because those are the first things the enemy tries to use against you. And nobody likes being seen as vulnerable to other people (this is where most competition comes from—weaknesses; areas in which we may be deficient). You have to learn how to take the low road sometimes. I've watched God many times over elevate me in ministry. Many instances where if I hadn't been focused the enemy would have distracted me, tricked me into giving into the people's choice instead of living up to God's choice.

One of Satan's most prized devices of deception is competition. This is what got him kicked out of heaven; jealousy led to competition, which caused him to challenge God. Big mistake. We too often look at what others are doing and how well they do what they do, that we get distracted and desire what God has for them—instead of what God has for us.

This is the spirit of a "Hater."

In sports you find this at astronomical levels, because competition is so thick. The East vs. the West, the Lakers vs. the Bulls. I mean, it doesn't stop and that's because competition is "never satisfied", there is no rest. But if you do things in the manner God would have you to do, you can find rest, and rest is good because it refreshes you for the next level. Matthew 11:29 says, "Take my yoke upon you, and *learn of me*; for I am meek and lowly in heart: and ye shall *find rest* unto your souls." While everyone else is sweating the competition, you're somewhere resting in God knowing that he's got your back!

As you begin to train and discipline yourself; as you challenge yourself to improve upon the gift, talent and abilities in you; as you perfect your craft, you eliminate competition; you don't need it. As a matter of fact, there are zero findings of the word "competition or compete" in the Bible. 2 Peter 1:10 says, "Wherefore the rather, brethren, give diligence to make your calling and election sure: for if ye do these things, ye shall never fall:" So many people have not made their calling and election sure, they have not committed to the purpose in their own lives; so they begin to covet what God has called someone else to in life...BIG MISTAKE.

Let's go to the scripture. In the Sixth Chapter of Daniel we learn that Daniel was preferred above presidents and princes because he possessed an excellent spirit in him. The king thought to set him over the whole realm of His kingdom. Sometimes in life you get ahead not only because you are gifted, but because you have the right *spirit*. I teach the members of my church and those I minister to abroad that my definition of a Spirit of Excellence is giving the anointing of God something to work with. Often times we desire opportunity but without the right spirit in which to receive it. Daniel would pray three times a day and was consistent. He knew the works of the Lord and what level he was responsible for and therefore disciplined himself likewise. When the enemy (*haters*) sees that you are disciplined and anointed too, they are powerless against that which worketh in you. It promotes you, it recommends you, it vouches for you, it opens doors for you, it destroys the yoke of competition in your midst.

WIN SOME, LOSE SOME

"And every one that hath forsaken houses, or brethren,
or sisters, or father, or mother, or wife, or children, or lands,
for my name's sake, shall receive an hundredfold,
and shall inherit everlasting life." — Matthew 19:29

This book is written about a strategy for success. You would think that a book about success would in no shape, form, or fashion have a chapter that discusses losing. As odd as it may seem, losing is very much a part of winning in any life of success. You cannot have one without the other—that is, if you're talking about true success. Uncle Governor says, "What makes south, south is north. What makes east, east is west; therefore, what makes success, success are failures."

In every sport, there are thrills of victory and the agony of defeat, that's all a part of the game. From the Super Bowl to the NBA Playoffs, from MLB World Series to the Olympic games, there are teams of athletes who can write their own book on the experience of winning some and losing some. Heywood Broun said, "Sports do not build character. They reveal it." Character is not just who people see in the game with the lights, cameras and crowded venues, but it's also off the court, on the sidelines and behind closed doors. It's not what happens if you lose, it's what happens when you lose.

A true definition of success includes failure. If all of us who live successful lives are honest, we have to say that much of our success came with great and dreadful losses. Some losses we had control over and others were out of our hands, but they made us better. As I stated previously that in life, it takes a good sport to accept a loss; especially when success slips through your own hands. But we can look at it from a positive perspective to understand that sometimes "losing keeps you fresh for winning". If you have never suffered a loss, if you have never failed at anything, you wouldn't have what it take to define success if it slapped you in the face.

In sports, there are teams we call the "underdogs". Underdogs are teams or individuals who are not expected to come out on top because of their track record of losses. Some teams go years with a track record of losing to the point where their "fans" are no longer cheering them on but booing them off the field. As the underdog, you have the odds stacked against you. Everything about you says "Loser." But for some apparent reason, it's the underdogs we root for, and are excited for when they come out on top. Something about the struggle, makes the victory even sweeter!

1 Corinthians 15:57-58 says, "But thanks be to God, which giveth us the victory through our Lord Jesus Christ. Therefore, my beloved brethren, be ye stedfast, unmoveable, always abounding in the work of the Lord, forasmuch as ye know that your labour is not in vain in the Lord."

We lose a lot of stuff (time, money, spouses, children, careers) because we fail to do what we do *in* the Lord and *for* the Lord. We cannot have superficial motives and expect God to favor our choices in life. When the superficial is your guide, all you are doing are stacking up your losses for a great fall. But whatever you do with a foundation of God will give you the victory.

We have to learn to include Him.

So how do you really deal with a loss? I mean, some losses are more damaging and detrimental than others. Many of us have found ourselves in life or death situations that if it had not been for the Lord who was on our side, where would we be? Many of us would be homeless, walking the streets, depressed and oppressed beyond measure. We would have lost our minds or would have been found serving out a death sentence. God has already defeated the darkness of life through His son Jesus, even death that we may live! The enemy will try to discourage you with fiery darts to make you disheartened, but we can rest assured that someone bigger than you and I, bigger than any problem we face, can fix everything going wrong in our lives. The blessed thing is that being in covenant with God, we experience a peace that "passeth all understanding" (Philippians 4:7) in that God is in control. This means that in every area of our, He has fixed it for us to triumph.

"Now thanks be unto God, which always causeth us to triumph in Christ, and maketh manifest the savour of his knowledge by us in every place." — 2 Corinthians 2:14

Let's meditate on this passage of scripture to get the real essence of what it is saying. The writer starts out with the idea of presently having an attitude of gratitude. In every state or situation you find yourself in, you should be thankful. The bible tells us "in" all things, not "for" all things give thanks. We should be thankful unto God. Guess what? It could be worse.

It goes on to tell us that He "causeth us to triumph". This is huge. God, in His infinite wisdom and power purposed victory for us regardless of the circumstance. He has already, by design, mandated the game be in our favor. All we have to do is trust Him, be obedient to His will and give thanks.

The latter part of this verse states His ability to know us in every place. Every hurdle you've run into, God already knew you would hit. This scripture is to encourage you with what you're struggling with today. God has your back! Don't throw in the towel, help is on the way.

Food for thought and consideration, God created us in His likeness, meaning that we are three parts being (body, soul and spirit). Therefore, as a result of this, God, by design, has already fixed it from the beginning for us to be whole, complete, well balanced and live victorious in all three areas. He's given man victory through Christ Jesus in every place. You were not created unstable without balance. You are not to be down trodden in life but you are to have dominion in life. Imagine... you are a triathlon winner by design! God has created you to triumph in body, soul and spirit. He's given you this victory and you win hands down. You have to be strong in the Lord and in the power of His might as He manifests himself in you through purpose. Learning from a loss can redefine you and make you a better person. Success appreciates learned losses because they are the inroads to purpose and purpose fulfills destiny!

If I were to define for you the meaning of a loss it would be detriment, disadvantage, damage, or trouble. Some things are good to lose and some things are even better to have never been gained, meaning that it separates you from the greater purpose God has intended for your life. After you experience hardship because of a hard head, you better understand to just leave some things alone. The bible puts it best in Mark 8:36, "for what shall it profit a man, if he shall gain the whole world, and <u>lose</u> his soul?" This simply lets us know that some things are not worth having or losing. We all would like a new car and a new house, new sports contract, new job and so on, but not everything is good for us and we should learn to appreciate the life God has for us. Now that's good living—when you can be thankful for what God has already given you knowing that He's not through blessing you yet.

We often get things twisted and look at things from the wrong perspective but the fact of the matter is that we should lose all negative thoughts and actions that obstruct our progress in living a productive life of success. Become proactive in speaking positively over your life and watch your outcome change.

For over a year or more my whole world seemed to be turned upside down. It was like I had wrecked my car on the Indy 500 and just kept flipping over and over. Everything you can imagine in my life seemed to have crashed and burned. We've all had a few knocks and bumps but I felt like I had been thrown down to the ground and had the wind knocked out of me. I experienced multiple losses in more than one area of my life. It would have been okay if I had to jump one hurdle at a time but not five or more at the same time.

Let me explain. The enemy now has changed his game plan of attack to match our multitasking culture of today. The enemy no longer attacks with one hit at a time; now he multitasks; he steals, kills and destroys all at the same time! I mean, full court press. There was a season in my life when I experienced this first hand.

My wife and I went through a dark period where hope sounded like a cliché; a very grim place of despair. It all started with the loss of my fulltime job and my part-time job within days of each other; then the wife lost her job as well. Neither of us received any unemployment benefits or public assistance. We were declined food stamps because they went by my previous year's income, which didn't help my present distress. For 14 months, with two children, there was no assistance. Let's keep moving.

Then our vehicle was repossessed twice, once from the church parking lot while my wife was leading praise and worship and I had to preach. We had to get a ride home from one of the saints. How embarrassing.

Then our home, located in the "Mexico" hood with high crime and drugs all around us, went into foreclosure; I mean if you can't survive living in the hood where else is there to go from here?

Okay, as if that wasn't enough, the enemy came back with a much harder punch. My wife had a miscarriage; probably stress related due to the pressures of life. And the enemy tried to another devilish distraction commonly called "who's to blame." Remember, my wife and I are in ministry. We encourage everyone else that God can make away, He's able and there's nobody like Jesus when these things occurred. But we know when the devil strikes hard, it's hard to hold onto those truths. And still things didn't slow down while our faith warred with these losses.

For those who read the dedication, within the same year, I lost two of the most influential people in my life, my "Uncle Breeze" and my Grandmother Willa. My grandmother, who lived to be 92, transformed my life at an early age. She taught me more than religion, she showed me how to have a Christian *relationship* with God. I told those who attended her homegoing that it would have been okay if she was "just grandmother" but that lady was more to me than that. She was heavenly placed in my life to instill the much needed character-building traits of a leader. And Uncle Breeze taught me everything I know about being a man, from how to be sharp in a suit to how to conduct myself with a lady. These were not just people, they were institutions in my life.

I was already wrestling, trying to hold "things" together but then I lost individuals who had helped mold me, those to whom I could always turn to in times of trouble for solid advice. This was too much. I began to break, to lose the very fabric of my faith... my mind. I had anxiety attacks, nightmares. I was fighting depression.

I couldn't understand what was happening to me. God had warned me in the prior year that I was going to have to trust Him but I thought this "trust" was going to be a casual thing. This was not what I was expecting. I mean, material things you

can always obtain but the death of valuable God sent people—
That blow was devastating.

I was also transitioning spiritually, growing and doing
more ministry than I ever had.

That's how we survived.

People called from out of the woodworks, asking me to
come minister in one form or fashion. God put it on my heart to
engage our community here in Alton, Illinois in what was at
the time the largest event I've led called Sunset Concerts. This
idea was borrowed from my college days Southern Illinois University (SIUC), where the Sunset Concerts were six-weeks of
secular music on the college campus we called "the yard". Now
saved and living for Christ, I wanted to impact the entire community with the idea of having mini concerts once a week,
showcasing a different genre of gospel music (rap & rock,
praise & worship, quartet, soloist, instrumentalist, etc.) for a
total of six weeks free to the public downtown at our newly
built Riverfront Amphitheatre. This was BIG!

My wife and I worked tirelessly to get this off the ground.
And our efforts were rewarded. We had suffered great losses,
but God immensely blessed us with much success. Over the six
weeks of concerts, we had an attendance of over 1,200 people!
While we took care of God's business, God to care of our business.

We have not recovered all and still struggle to regain some
of what was lost, but we understand God's word to be true. We
trust God. In the midst of all these trials, God blessed me to
start work again in my field of study as a Mechanical Design
Engineer in Greenville, IL. As a sign that God was still present
with me, the building where I was to work was located between
two streets, Washington (wife's maiden name) and Harris (yep,
that's my name). This was my confirmation that the job was
mine...it had my name all on it! In addition to this I made histo-

ry as the first African-American Engineer this sports company has ever had since its inception in over 85 years plus. Psalm 23 says, "Surely goodness and mercy shall follow me all the days of my life and I will dwell in the house of the Lord for ever." I was in the right place, doing the right thing and serving the right God! God will allow you not only to be successful but he will allow you to make history.

This seemed to have angered the enemy so much; he quit attacking the things around me or connected to me and started attacking my physical body. I've noticed that the enemy attacks the body as a last resort (remember Job). This is what he did to me. I began to get sick. I was running myself down, providing for family and ministering as the newly installed pastor of Brown's Faith Temple COGIC church.

The family and I were headed to my son's drum lessons in St. Louis and I felt unusually sick. The truck ran out of gas and there we were stranded on the side of the highway after crossing a neighboring bridge in St. Louis. I was so hot and had nothing to drink. I began to have shortness of breath. I became so overwhelmed with heat that my clothes stuck to me like glue. I became incoherent and light headed. I felt that I was going to pass out. I rushed to get under the shade of bushes. My phone died, and my wife went to find help. No one would stop, except a man who left once he saw me lying helpless in the bushes. My head was hurting, my mouth was dry. My heart began to race as I felt my life was slowly being drained from my body.

The only thing I could do was repeat Psalms 27:13 over and over, "I had fainted, unless I had believed to see the goodness of the Lord in the land of the living."

By the grace of God one of my wife's friends, Lexie, was headed to pick up her daughter from St. Louis and stopped to help. Lexie was truly a lifesaver.

You have to believe that the goodness of the Lord is for you while you are yet on this side of heaven. I know you've been running for a long time trying to make one hundred, I know you've been racing against the clock trying to make up for lost time from Satan's setbacks. Understand this, *God has you* and if you hang in there—don't throw in the towel, don't faint, don't pass out—the favor of God is coming to your rescue!

You see, many times we don't see the hand of God or listen to the voice of God, so when we face things of this magnitude, it seems impossible to recover from such great losses. As you may already know our American society is tore up from the floor up! Everything from our economy to the family has lost its value and is at death's door, but we've got to keep the faith, because this too will pass.

It is hard to say to have the strength and courage to say as the Shunammite woman did, after the prophet of God promised her a son and he later died, "It is well" (2 Kings 4:8-37) or in today's terms, "It's all good." We may be faced with grave choices, some do or die decisions but we have to look at it with the glass half full perspective. Since everything is on the down, there's nowhere to go but up. When things are already rock bottom in your life, by building a strong foundation in God through His word, you can't do anything but start going up.

While writing this book, I found myself unemployed, but it was a blessing in disguise in that I was able to allow God to put the pieces of my life back together for the next move God would have me make. We don't understand how things work but we must trust God. I'm in a place now where I'm thankful for every door that closes because God has another door waiting for us to go through. I'm thankful to God in that one of the best things that could have happened to me was for my employer to let me go. God used that to motivate me to get into position.

He's able to provide for us regardless of what our environment is saying to us. In one of my sermons, I delivered a message entitled "That's for the Birds" from 1 Kings 17. God commanded the prophet Elijah, after he prophesied of the famine in the land, to go down to the brook Cherith. There he would cause ravens to feed him. Elijah was obedient to the voice of the Lord. And the Lord was sure to His word. See, God will always provide for His people, we just have to be obedient to the voice of the Lord, even when He is directing us to do something that doesn't make sense to our sensibility. You don't have to worry about your problems in life, leave it to the birds, you just praise and thank God because little becomes much when you place it in the Master's hands.

One of the most catastrophic events in American history was the attack on the World Trade Centers in New York City. Never in the history of the United States had we experienced such a loss: over 3,000 lives gone, commerce activity crushed and for some a loss of hope. But we who are believers understand that our hope is in the Lord and Savior Jesus Christ who maketh us not ashamed concerning the things of our faith (Romans 5:5).

The enemy, al-Qaeda, was responsible for the attack on the World Trade Center, the Pentagon and another flight headed toward the White House that crashed in Pennsylvania. The whole country, if not the whole world, watched as the very fabric of our lives dissipated... hope snuffed. This is how the enemy, the devil, has done so many of us, in attacking us in different areas of lives all at the same time because he comes only but to kill, steal and destroy. He knows and sees that an isolated attack here and there merely slows you down.

He will attack and deplete your finances. Then if that doesn't work he'll hit your marriage. He will follow up with an attack on your job through a lay-off. And if worse comes to worst, he will afflict your body with cancer, diabetes, stroke, or a heart attack.

He likes pulling out all the stops in a full fledge assault. Nevertheless, we cannot allow what looks bad or feels bad to prohibit the progress of us doing better than what our circumstances are saying to us. Our greatest president of my lifetime and probably in the history of our country, Barak Obama authored the best seller *The Audacity of Hope*, his thoughts on reclaiming the American Dream. But the reality of the American Dream is more than the push of tangible success gained in life, but the power of God through our passion and purpose that drives you from an American *Dream* to the reality of your destiny.

Faith is our audacity to hope; it is the "right now" active ingredient to our future. Hebrews 11:1 says, "Now faith is the substance of things hoped for it is the evidence of things not seen." Our faith in God allows us to see in dark places, it's our night vision. Psalms 119 says, "He is a lamp unto my feet and a light unto our path", so keep your head up and know that weeping may endure for a night but joy comes in the morning.

A decade after the fall of the Twin Towers, America was still rebuilding, not what was but what is to be, a future downtown New York City that would be a memorial in honor of those who lost their lives—a single world trade center tower to stand tall and proud in the face of our adversaries. From the grounds of the once mangled buildings, a monument of serenity rises from the ashes. We are to be like this tower, the once twin towers symbolically represented an image of togetherness and the need for support, but when you've been through hell and back and have survived all the devil's many attacks, you can stand alone and say to the world, *In your face!*

We are more than a conqueror through Christ Jesus who strengthens us and greater is He that is in us than he that is in the world. You have the freedom to explore and soar, nothing can stop you because you are not relying upon your own strength but the Lord's. Scripture has it that the joy of the Lord is our strength, so understand how to get excited about the trials and tribulations that come your way because in giving thanks to God you can stand the tests of time.

I know that it may sound strange to hear but we often take a loss the wrong way. The scripture says that, "all things work together for the good of them that love the Lord" so everything that we face and encounter works for us, those who are the called according to His purpose. Even our losses have a place in helping us fulfill our destiny. Success isn't success without losses. If you take your losses in stride and learn from them, it keeps you fresh for winning. You cannot win every game or championship, you win some and you lose some... just make sure you learn from the losses and lean on God.

Commitment to Walk in God's Wisdom and Plan

Father, I thank You that the communication of my faith becomes effectual by acknowledging every good thing which is in me in Christ Jesus. I hear the voice of the Good Shepherd. I hear my Father's voice, and the voice of a stranger I will not follow.

Father, I believe in my heart and say with my mouth that this day the will of God is done in my life. I walk in a manner worthy of You, Lord, desiring to please You in all things, bearing fruit in every good work. Jesus wisdom has been revealed unto me. I single-mindedly walk in that wisdom expecting to know what to do in every situation and to be on top of every circumstance!

I give my works unto You, Lord. Make my thoughts agreeable to Your will, so my plans are established and will succeed. Direct my steps and make them sure. I understand and firmly grasp what the will of the Lord is for I am not vague, thoughtless, or foolish. I stand firm and mature in spiritual growth, convinced and fully assured in everything willed by God.

Father, You have destined and appointed me to come progressively to know Your will—to recognize more strongly and clearly, and to become better and more intimately acquainted with Your will. I thank You, Father, for the Holy Spirit who abides permanently in me and who guides me into Your truth—the whole, full Truth—and speaks whatever He hears from the Father and announces and declares to me the things that are to come. Father, let me have the mind of Christ and hold the thoughts, feelings, and purposes of His heart.

Father, I have entered into that blessed rest by adhering, trusting, and relying on You in the name of Jesus.

Hallelujah!

Scripture References

Philemon 6
John 10:5
Colossians 4:12
John 10:27
Ephesians 5:17
Acts 22:14
Philippians 4:8

PART 2: PRACTICE — STRATEGIES

"[F]or bodily exercise profiteth little; but godliness is profitable unto all things, having promise of the life that now is, and of that which is to come." –1 Timothy 4:8

Everything up until now was an introduction to the strategies that are made for success. You need tactics and not semantics to get you from point A to point B in life. Strategies are God given principles for purpose in your life. In the times we live, it takes principles to fight against the principalities that wage war against our finances, our families and our future (Ephesians 6:12). We have to know what we're up against when we are pushed into the corner so that, with the help of God, we can get off the ropes of life and start fighting again. You must be courageous enough to challenge all contenders that oppose the purpose and destiny God has outlined for you.

Whether experiencing pressures internally or externally, you must find a way to get home court advantage. Sometimes our attacks come from the outside, people who have hurt you and situations you felt out of control to change. And sometimes from within, we are our own worst enemy, besieged by self doubt, self hate and self destruction. Restate your claim on life. Remind the enemy whose turf he's on! Psalms 24:1 reads, "For the earth is the Lord's and the fullness thereof; the world and they that dwell therein." You are a child of God. You are the head (first stream, starter) and not the tail (third stream, last on the bench). You are above (first draft) and not beneath (without a contract).

Open yourself up to a whole new world of success and watch God do great things in your life. Go for the gold!

Put your game face on and use strategy and kingdom tactics to get you the win!

SWING: SO WHAT I NEED GOD

"Everyone who calls on the name of the Lord will be saved."
—Romans 10:13

As the spiritual says, "swing low sweet chariot, coming for to carry me home." While this is a song of comfort and peace, it's also a song of movement, of action. In slavery days, enslaved Africans sneaking away by the North Star to freedom sang the song as a sign that the Underground Railroad conductor was on the way. It was a cry for help and a response that help was on the way to carry you from point A to point B. Help was on the way.

I can hear my mother singing, "Help Me...Help Me Lord. I Need Your Help...Help Me Lord". This call and response song is traditionally sung in "Testimony Service," in what we call "Praise & Worship." The song is a testament to others and God that we need Him. A recognition that we need God's help in our everyday lives. You know that the only way you're gonna make it is with the help of the Lord carrying you across the finish line. This place is a place of comfort that can only be understood after accepting God's peace through His salvation.

This peace usually comes not when you think you have already arrived, you've finally received the promotion you wanted, or after you've won the championship and have been the recipient of the MVP award. This peace comes when the electricity is off, the car repossessed, the home is in foreclosure, and you're in the unemployment line, sitting on the sideline with no championship trophy in hand. This peace usually comes right after you say to yourself, if I ever needed the Lord before, I sure do need Him now. Now I'm not talking about Tyler Perry and Madea's "piece", that's the wrong kind; I'm talking about the *peace of God that passeth all understanding.*

When situations and circumstances arise that challenge your confidence, say:

SO WHAT I NEED GOD!

This simple plea, if asked around the world, is the sentiment of many believers' hearts. Think about it; if it were not for the Lord who is on our side where would you be? We can do nothing of our own; it takes God himself to empower us with life, health and the strength to wake up every morning, let alone live a successful life. Deuteronomy 31:6 says, "Be strong and of a good courage, fear not, nor be afraid of them: for the Lord thy God, he it is that doth go with thee; he will not fail thee, nor forsake thee." Matthew 28:20 says, "...lo, I am with you always, even unto the end of the world." Now that's comfort and reliability!

If you don't understand the wiles of the devil you will fall captive to his snares and traps. The enemy gets many of us off track, thinking that we alone are the ones who, as they say in the streets, "do what it do." We must understand the scripture means what it says and says what it means when it says "Not by might, or by power, but by His spirit saith the Lord of host" (Zechariah 4:6). God strengthens us to start and finish our day. You have to remember that in Him we live, move and have our being. We can do all things through Christ who strengthens us. They say, if you don't stand for something, you will fall for anything. Stand on the Rock of Salvation and let the Lord work his wonders for you.

If God is for us, who can be against us?

We didn't create ourselves. We belong to God. We are His *most* prized possession. His trophy! Recognizing that we need God is humbling and places us in submission to the obedience of God's word. It also opens the door to whatever we need, because we are His children and He is our father; joint heirs with

Christ Jesus to both heaven and earth. It should be intuitive. Just face the fact. So what we all need God.

PUSH: Pray Until Something Happens

"Confess your faults one to another and pray one for another, that ye may be healed. The effectual fervent prayer of a righteous man availeth much." — James 5:16

Sometimes the game is such a loss that it appeared to be a thrown game. Who's to blame? Someone is responsible for us losing right? But no one ever wants to raise their hand or their voice to admit that as a team we've all fallen short of the glory of God.

There is a specific sound that only you can produce that God is looking to hear; a sound that breaks all barriers, a sound that penetrates all. When you pray it establishes relationship with God that resonates a willingness to stay connected. God likes nothing more than to stay connected to you, even when you've fallen short of his promises for your life, he's still there. Above the loud yells, screams and hissing, God still hears you. It's so easy to blame the next player on your team for the loss but sometimes it's our fault. We made the mistake, we erred, but that's okay. Confession is good for the soul. Confession in prayer is a strong tactic against the devil. It can only get you closer to both Him and your destiny! Matthew 6:9-13 outlines the prayer that Jesus taught His disciples, the "Lord's Prayer".

Our Father which art in heaven, Hallowed be thy name.
Thy kingdom come, Thy will be done in earth, as it is in heaven.
Give us this day our daily bread.
And forgive us our debts, as we forgive our debtors.
And lead us not into temptation, but deliver us from evil:
For thine is the kingdom and the power and the glory, for ever.
Amen.

The Lord's Prayer is a positioning statement of faith that allows the will of God to be done in every area of our lives; it is our platform to reach the Father. Prayer is the voice of faith. Prayer is the key and faith unlocks the door. Our forefathers in ministry taught us a simple concept—no prayer, no power; little prayer, little power; much prayer, much power.

I remember growing up as a young boy being taught that a good athlete is one who doesn't mind contact. A true sportsman understands that when you are on the field, you intend to get a little physical. But as a child in the little league, we were only allowed to play flag football—there was no contact. It was fun, but the victory was just as small as we were. When I got older, I joined a league where contact was allowed. Here the stakes are higher, you look to get hit or do the hitting. Then there is rugby.

Now, rugby is a different level of football—full body contact. Rugby is extreme. This level of football is played by the most skilled, gifted and talented; fearless in the knowledge that they have the power to knock your block off.

Isaiah 54:17 reads, "No weapon that is formed against thee shall prosper; and every tongue that shall rise against thee in judgment thou shalt condemn. This is the heritage of the servants of the Lord and their righteousness is of me, saith the Lord."

God has you covered! Like these rugby players, when you have trained in the ways of the Lord and you come to him diligently in prayer, he will give you the power to send the enemy packing. And if by chance the enemy hits you below the belt, leaving you speechless, know this: the Holy Spirit will work for you when you can't say a word. Romans 8:26-28 says:

"Likewise the Spirit also helpeth our infirmities (weaknesses): for we know not what we should pray for as we

ought: but the Spirit itself maketh intercession for us with groaning which cannot be uttered. And he that searcheth the hearts knoweth what is the mind of the Spirit, because he maketh intercession for the saints according to the will of God. And we know that all things work together for good to them that love God, to them who are called according to his purpose."

The enemy wants you to bite your tongue on every word of God that you profess over your life. But God's will for your life is not excruciating pain; it is the purpose in us that must be fulfilled. What you go through doesn't always feel good, but it works for your good. Uncle Governor taught me that everything we go through in life is "employed" by us to work for our good to fulfill the purpose of God in our lives (Romans 8:28). The divorce you've gone through, the job you lost, the unexpected doctor's report—this is all employed by you to work for your good. Yes, it's uncomfortable; you may have had the wind knocked out of you, but as sure as they were hired they can be fired and every attack by the enemy will be cancelled in the name of Jesus!

You have to learn to put your foot on the enemy's neck by opening up your mouth and speaking God's Word. There is power in the tongue and in the name of Jesus. Using your words wisely can touchdown places in your life that nothing else can reach. What makes us strong is using the name of the Lord Jesus. The bible says that His name is a strong tower into which the righteous run and are saved. Simply by saying His name demons are made to tremble and glory is given to God... now that's how you make contact.

SHOOT: START HELPING OTHERS...OFFER-TRUST

Then the LORD said to Cain, "Where is your brother Abel?"

"I don't know," he replied. "Am I my brother's keeper?"
–Genesis 4:9

There's always great debate over who the greatest shooter in basketball is. Is it Michael Jordan? Is it Kobe Bryant? How about Dr. Jay? We think that it's all about making the shot when there's a whole game that is played with teammates helping and assisting. The question is can you shoot?

The answer to that question is a resounding, YES! They say teamwork makes the dream work. However you look at it, you are blessed with the responsibility to consider helping someone else fulfill their purpose; it's an act of selflessness. Every sport has its objective to score points. Whether it's a goal, a par, or strike, we have to aim to get it. Aiming is so very important to your success. Everything you do in life should focus toward, be aimed at, your purpose and if your purpose is only "me and mine" then you probably won't get very far; and if you do, you will experience a loneliness that is unrewarding. Success involves not only yourself, but others. There will be a time when you need someone else and there is always an opportunity for you to lend a helping hand to others.

When you begin to think of others, you can and will achieve a greater level of success, far more rewarding than anything you can imagine. In life, it is important that we use wisdom to seize purposeful opportunities assisting others reach their goals. Not all things appear fruitful, but may be more profitable than they seem. It is quite clear that Michael Jordan, Larry Bird and Kobe Bryant, are icons in the sport of basketball. But guess what makes them an even better player are their ability to assist others in the game. That's how we all win in real life, by helping and assisting.

A good MVP does not act alone, nor does an MVP with integrity take all the credit. An MVP motivates the team to achieve the win. No man is an island. When the day is done, God requires us to help others reach their potential in living a successful life. Yes, it's true that you cannot help everyone but as the hymn says, "if I can help someone along the way then my living is not in vain". There can be no success without assistance somewhere along the way and that assistance is never in vain.

Think about it this way. We were all lost in sin and disconnected from God the Father. Christ Jesus came from heaven to earth, on earth to the cross, from the cross to the grave, from the grave to the sky on our behalf to save us and reconcile us back to God. In John 3:16, "For God so loved the world that he gave his only begotten Son, that whosoever believeth in Him should not perish (lose), but have everlasting life (win)." God gave us the pinnacle example of teamwork. He knew that we needed help and we were lost in our sins on our way to a devil's hell. There was nothing we could do to regain relationship with the Father; no money could purchase that, no sacrifice could have been offered that was good enough, no trophy could be won, nothing but the blood of Jesus! So he sent in the star player, His Son, to save the game and by grace we are now saved, all of us who accepts the help.

It is said that there are six degrees of separation, meaning that we are all connecting and are just six people away from each other. Can you imagine that we live in a world of over seven billion people and we are so very connected? We never know who we will come in contact with and how we will affect each other's lives, but one thing is for sure–the awesomeness of God who purposed us to coexist without ever colliding but edifying one another in the body of Christ. Now that's amazing. Who you are in God will never conflict with who I am in God. That's why there's no need to compete. It's not until we learn to acknowledge and celebrate the God in others that can we become productive ourselves. It takes nothing from any of us to work together; it's called support and collaborative efforts. God himself had three people involved with everything he created and formed—God the Father, God the Son and God the Holy Spirit. Romans 12:5 says, "So we, being many, are one body in Christ and every one members one of another," meaning even while having our own separate roles, we are joined and connected together to edify the body of Christ. We must recognize our obligation and responsibility that we have toward one another because God requires that if we love Him, we must also love one another. "Jesus said unto him, Thou shalt love the Lord thy God with all thy heart and with all thy soul and with all thy mind. This is the first and great commandment. And the second is like unto it, Thou shalt love thy neighbour as thyself. On these two commandments hang all the law and the prophets." (Matthew 22:36-40).

Often times we who have found our purpose and are living a successful life, forget that there are others who are on the same course as you are. We allow the enemy to get in our minds to refrain ourselves in helping someone else as if by doing so you will lose your place or position. But God's plan for your life doesn't collide with any other, it may simply overlap. We have to position ourselves to "coach and not roast" someone. This simple means that when you see someone with a similar goal or vision, don't step on their dreams, don't deal with the devil by derailing their destiny. God gave us dominion and he commanded us to multiply ourselves and be fruitful. What better way to multiply yourself then through someone else?

What better way to be fruitful then by seeding into someone else?

"Each One Teach One." I was taught that once you have the understanding of the material good enough to teach someone else, then you really have the goods and teaching increases your own ability to master the material. Find someone into whom you can pour and seed favor. This keeps you sharp and on top of your game.

Jesus was asked by His disciples what is the most important rule that they needed to obey to inherit the kingdom of God (heaven) and Jesus being who he is simply replied to them that all the law hang on this one concept which is to love thy neighbor as yourself. This passage of scripture is so very significant but many of us miss the heart of the matter at hand. We, like the disciples, always want to know the bottom line, what it is that we need to do in order to get the promotion, close on the new house, make the team and score the winning point. But more importantly we should consider the words Jesus explained to the disciples which are we should love your neighbor as *yourself*. This literally means that in order for you to reach your goal, you have to start thinking of others as you do yourself. Think about it, if you like nice things, if you desire a prosperous and flourishing life, if you train with the best to be the best, why not help others who are likeminded? If you love who you are in God and what He has made you to become, if you like how success feels, than you will love the God in someone else and see how you can help them to become successful too.

WILLIAM C. HARRIS

Commitment to Pray and Practice

Father, in the name of Jesus, I offer up thanksgiving that You have called me to be a fellow workman—a joint promoter and a laborer together—with and for You. I commit myself to pray and not to turn coward – faint, lose heart, or give up.

Fearlessly and confidently and boldly I draw near to the throne of grace that I may receive mercy and find grace to help in good time for every need—appropriate help and well-timed help, coming just when I (and others) need it. This is the confidence that I have in You, that, if I ask anything according to Your will, You hear me: and if I know that You hear me, whatsoever I ask, I know that I have the petitions that I desired of You.

When I do not know what prayer to offer and how to offer it worthily as I ought, I thank You, Father, that the Spirit comes to my aid and bears me up in my weakness, in my inability to produce results. He, the Holy Spirit, goes to meet my supplication and pleads in my behalf with unspeakable yearnings and groanings too deep for utterance. And He Who searches the hearts of men knows what is in the mind of the Spirit. The Holy Spirit intercedes and pleads in behalf of the saints according to and in harmony with God's will. Therefore, I am assured and know that God being a partner in my labor, all things work together and are fitting into a plan for my good, because I love God and am called according to His design and purpose.

I do not fret or have any anxiety about anything, but in every circumstance and in everything by prayer and petition (definite requests) with thanksgiving continue to make my wants and the wants of others known to God. Whatever I ask for in prayer, I believe that it is granted to me, and I will receive it.

The earnest (heartfelt, continued) prayer of a righteous man makes tremendous power available—dynamic in its working. Father, I live in You—abide vitally united to You—and Your words remain in me and continue to live in my heart. Therefore, I ask whatever I will and it shall be done for me. When I bear (produce) much fruit (through prayer), You, Father, are honored and glorified. Hallelujah!

Scripture References

Psalms 34
Ephesians 6:12
1 Corinthians 3:9 AMP
1 John 5:14,15
Mark 11:24 AMP
Luke 18:1 AMP
Romans 8:26-29 AMP
James 5:16b AMP
Hebrews 4:16 AMP
Philippians 4:6 AMP
John 15:7,8 AMP

PART 3: PURPOSE – YOUR MISSION FOR SUCCESS

"Make you perfect in every good work to do his will, working in
you that which is well pleasing in his sight, through Christ Jesus;
to whom be glory for ever and ever. Amen." — Hebrews 12:21

You have learned about vision, you've considered your diet and have begun watching your weight, you've learned to implement steps that lead to a productive and successful life by eliminating competition, maximizing your impact through simple strategies—SWING, PUSH and SHOOT—so what's next?

God's heart desire from the beginning was to make you perfect in every good work to do his will. Again, you are his greatest trophy through Christ Jesus, therefore your mission for success must be fulfilled. You now recognize your gifts, talents, skills and abilities, but what are you doing with them?

I once preached a message "What On Earth Are You Doing?" The basis for this message comes from the parable found in the synoptic gospels of the story about the Talents. There were three servants that the master invested talents into, one had five talents, one had two talents and the third one had one talent. Two out of the three servants worked their talents while the one who had one talent buried his talent in the earth. Is this servant you? Have you buried what God has gifted you to do on earth, stuck it in the ground somewhere and never profited from the talent? When the master came back to see his investment of talents with the servants, two out the three were rewarded double the amount of their initial talent; however, the third servant who had buried his one gift was stripped of that talent and cast into outer darkness. This is simply lights out, everyone has gone home leaving you in the park, on the court, in the field alone without anything to show because you failed to get in the game and use what God gave you. This servant lost everything he was given because he did not trust what God had given him.

Remember, if you be faithful over a few things, God will make you ruler of many!

NEGOTIATING THE CONTRACT: PRICELESS

"For our light affliction, which is but for a moment, worketh for
us a far more exceeding and eternal weight of glory."
— 2 Corinthians 4:17

As post-modern believers, we easily observe many secular persons who live for money, cars and clothes but these are merely objects with a price tag, but what we have in Christ Jesus is priceless. Yes, I said it, priceless. Don't sell out—be *souled out*! The opening scripture says it all. The hardships and difficulties that we face in this present life are considered light afflictions that are just for a moment in time. All of the pain from training and practice lasts only for a season but the payoff is much better than gold—for praising Him, God returns the glory!

God's glory in your life is more valuable than the weight of all the Olympic golds ever won. 2 Corinthians 4:18 says, "While we look not at the things which are seen, but at the things which are not seen: for the things which are seen are temporal; but the things which are not seen are eternal." All the trials and tribulations faced here on earth are temporary (divorce, debt, disease) but the things not seen (love, joy and peace with God) are forever. If we are in right-standing with God, we have eternal success. Priceless.

It's interesting how God works in giving you ideas that are bigger than yourself. Romans 11:33 explains, "O the depth of the riches both of the wisdom and knowledge of God and how unsearchable are His ways and His ways past finding out." Everything that we need to live on "top of the world" is in Him, the Almighty. As we make attempts to learn about our Savior and look for ways to please God with the gifts, talents and abilities He's given us, we will see how rich and successful our lives can become in Him.

Never allow the enemy to trick you into selling yourself cheap, you are very valuable to God. You are in God's thoughts and He has incredible ideas surrounding the success of you. It was God the Father, God the Son and God the Holy Ghost that said let us make man in our likeness and image and He breathed into man's nostrils and we became a living soul. Remember that God *gave His only begotten Son* that whosoever believes in Him will have eternal life; that's expensive.

Regardless of what others may think about you or what you think about yourself—and sometimes we are our worst critics—we have to get past it to see what God thinks about us. We are fearful and wonderfully made.

Your Mission

It's unnerving how many individuals do not see themselves living a better life in the future than what they are now. You have to know without a shadow of a doubt that there is a greater YOU ahead, you are God's prized trophy! You may not see it but the devil himself perceives it. The enemy knows that if he can magnify the problem he can cause you to miss your promise, so he tries 24/7 to throw our perception off to the point of giving up and quitting.

You have to understand the Power of Perception. Much of what we go through in life begins in our mind and spirit before it ever enters the atmosphere or environment; but God has not given us a spirit of fear but power, love and a sound mind. Once you begin to apply the God given faith, even the small size of a mustard seed, you can begin to move mountains in your life and help others to do the same. Mountains of fear, doubt, anxiety, loneliness, unforgiveness and more.

God has given us power over all the works of the enemy. Romans 8:37-39 says:

"Nay, in all these things we are more than conquerors through him that loved us. For I am persuaded, that neither death, or life, or angels, or principalities, or powers, or things present, or things to come, or height, or depth, or any other creature, shall be able to separate us from the love of God, which is in Christ Jesus our Lord".

This is the power of perception, knowing that everything the enemy throws your way has to become subject to the Will of God. Many of us will never be MVP athletes at the professional

67

level; most of us will never have the opportunity to play before thousands of fans; but we who are on God's team have the entire host of heaven watching us win against all odds in every area of our lives.

When working out, many people become discouraged because they can't seem to find the inner strength and discipline to be consistent. Sometimes we need an accountability partner, who fulfills scripture by being our keeper, helping us through this journey called life. God already gave us the best assist—Jesus. And Jesus sent the Comforter, the Holy Spirit, who will never leave us, or forsake us, but will be with us until the ends of the world. You have the best life coaches possible that money can't buy.

After Jesus completed His mission, He had a few more words in Him that we, as His disciples should live by—the "Great Commission". Jesus said:

> *"Go ye into all the world and preach the gospel to every creature. He that believeth and is baptized shall be saved; but he that believeth not shall be damned. And these signs shall follow them that believe; In my name shall they cast out devils; they shall speak with new tongues; They shall take up serpents; and if they drink any deadly thing, it shall not hurt them; they shall lay hands on the sick and they shall recover. So then after the Lord had spoken unto them, he was received up into heaven and sat on the right hand of God. And they went forth and preached every where, the Lord working with them and confirming the word with signs following. Amen." (Mark 16:15-16).*

We are responsible for saving our own souls and helping others come to the light. God, through His Son Jesus, has given us power over all the works of the enemy; there's no harm that he can ultimately do to us when we do the will of the Father. Satan gave it his best shot throwing everything he had at Jesus while on earth; even the cross. But nothing worked because Jesus said in Matthew 16 "not my will but your will be done". The will of the Father is for us all to be saved which is real success! 2 Peter 3:9 says, "The Lord is not slack concerning his promise, as some men count slackness; but is longsuffering to us-ward, not willing that any should perish, but that all should come to repentance." We become successful doing the will of the Father.

Mission is the act or an instance of sending; a ministry commissioned by a religious organization to propagate its faith or carry on humanitarian work; a specific task with which a person or a group is charged. Are you charged up in your faith? Are you willing to go the distance?

Acts 26:15-18 says:

"And I said, Who art thou, Lord? And he said, I am Jesus whom thou persecutest. But rise, and stand upon thy feet: for I have appeared unto thee for this purpose, to make thee a minister and a witness both of these things which thou hast seen, and of those things in the which I will appear unto thee; Delivering thee from the people, and from the Gentiles, unto whom now I send thee, To open their eyes, and to turn them from darkness to light, and from the power of Satan unto God, that they may receive forgiveness of sins, and inheritance among them which are sanctified by faith that is in me."

God wants to save us from ourselves and from the works of the enemy so that we can be examples to others that he connects us to on our jobs, on the court or field, in the gym, at the store, at church, and in our homes. He wants to empower us with success to shine in a very dark world!

69

GETTING TO THE FINISH LINE

"For I know the thoughts that I think toward you, saith the Lord, thoughts of peace, and not of evil, to give you an expected end." —
Jeremiah 29:11

Finishing is good and a real BIG thing to God.

Paul, a servant in bonds to God through Christ Jesus, proclaimed that He had "fought a good fight," and that Jesus had <u>finished</u> his course (2 Timothy 4:7). It's not until we fulfill our purpose in God do we receive a "well done, thy good and faithful servant" (Matthew 25:23).

Finishing is just as important as starting, if not more important. If man's existence started with God, don't you think it's only right to end up with God? I told you that God created and made us after His own likeness and that Jesus is the author and the finisher of our faith.

Never allow the enemy to dictate your outcome.

You have to step away from your work and ask yourself the question, am I fulfilling my purpose, my mission? Because if you're not fulfilling your purpose, you have a slim chance of being successful. I pray that you answer the call as Jesus did. Jesus understood, "not my will but your will be done".

When we see things adversely affecting our lives, apply faith to counter attack the enemy. Faith positions us with God and puts us in agreement with the Will of God for our lives, no matter what our past or present circumstance looks like. Faith says to the enemy that he is powerless. It is through faith that kingdoms are subdued, righteousness is worked and promises are obtained; yes, promises are obtained! Anyone who has ever experienced any level of success always started and finished with faith. The only thing about faith is that you cannot wait to use it, it is a "NOW" thing (read Hebrews 11). It works for your present distress. Faith not used is faith wasted.

So here's the secret to success that has been around since before the foundations of the world...

God!

Since the foundations of the world, God has been whispering the answer to man, first up close (*in the garden*) and after man sinned, from a distance, but he never stopped speaking about strategizes to success. Uncle Governor pointed out to me once how many of us mess up words in songs and totally change the meaning of it all together. There's a song that we sing and many of us would say "<u>til</u> he speaks from eternity" but the song actually says "*still* he speaks from eternity". God is not through with you or mankind, he still speaks from eternity concerning the purpose He has for our lives and is not waiting on anything but you to hear him out. He's at the sideline (eternity) coaching the next move in your life right now. Respond, answer the call, make the play. We have to live a God-centered life. Our forefathers would sing a song that sums it up perfectly, "There is *no secret* what God can do; what He's done for others; He'll do the same thing for you". The secret is out and He's been trying to get your attention from day one. Don't you hear Him calling you even now? He has purpose in you. He's the God that changes not; "he's the same today, yesterday and forever more" (Hebrews 13:8).

"Every good gift and every perfect gift is from above and cometh down from the Father of lights, with whom is no variableness, neither shadow of turning." — James 1:17

When you reach a certain level in math you begin to deal with variables. These variables are the unknown answers to the problems you are solving. God is the answer to your solution; He is making himself known to you, to handle everything concerning you and your purpose so that you reach your destiny with no variables. Think of it this way. God cannot fail us or lie to us; these are two things God cannot do. This is why we must seek His will for our lives to be successful because He has the answers to all of our questions.

Who do I need to talk with about this idea?

When should I make the next move?

Where do I go to get help?

The answers are all found in God!

Uncle Governor, my mentor, taught me that God is the only one who can send you somewhere, be with you on the journey to the place that He's sending you, and be there when you get there. I'm convinced that God will bring you unto your expected end; He will give you a commandment of covenant (promise), grant you a just (worthwhile) journey of peace that surpasses all of your understanding, and a place of providence (purpose) and destiny. There is none, like Him.

Anyone who knows anything about marathons knows that a good runner has endurance; strength is good, being swift is good, but lasting the distance is even better; this means you have the power to finish. The Bible encourages us to know that the race is not given to the strong or to the swift but to the one that endures until the end. All you are responsible for is signing up, getting your number and running. Run to finish the race.

Commitment to Purpose, Equipped for Success

Father, I thank You that the entrance of Your words gives light. I thank You that Your Word which You speak (and which I speak) is alive and full of power – making it active, operative, energizing, and effective. I thank You, Father, that {You have given me a spirit} of power, and of love, and of a calm and well-balanced mind, and discipline, and self-control. I have Your power and ability and sufficiency, for You have qualified me (making me to be fit and worthy and sufficient) as a minister and dispenser of a new covenant {of salvation through Christ}.

In the name of Jesus, I walk out of the realm of failure into the arena of success, giving thanks to You, Father, for You have qualified and made me fit to share the portion which is the inheritance of the saints (God's holy people) in the Light.

Father, You have delivered and drawn me to Yourself out of the control and the dominion of darkness (failure, doubt and fear) and have transferred me into the Kingdom of the Son of Your love, in Whom there is good success [and freedom from fears, agitating passions, and moral conflicts]. I rejoice in Jesus Who has come that I might have life and have it more abundantly.

Today I am a new creation, for I am (ingrafted) in Christ, the Messiah. The old (previous moral and spiritual condition) has passed away. Behold, the fresh and new has come! I forget those things which are behind me and reach forth unto those things which are before me. I am crucified with Christ: nevertheless I live; yet not I, but Christ lives in me: and the life which I now live in the flesh I live by the faith of the Son of God, Who loved me, and gave Himself for me.

Today I attend to the Word of God. I consent and submit to Your sayings, Father. Your words shall not depart from my sight; I will keep them in the midst of my heart with all vigilance and above all that I guard, for out of it flow the springs of life.

Today I will not let mercy and kindness and truth forsake me. I bind them about my neck; I write them upon the tablet of my heart. So therefore I will find favor, good understanding, and high esteem in the sight [or judgement] of God and man.

Today my delight and desire are in the law of the Lord, and on His law I habitually meditate (ponder and study) by day and by night. Therefore I am like a tree firmly planted [and tended] by the streams of water, ready to bring forth my fruit in my season; my leaf also shall not fade or wither, and everything I do shall prosper [and come to maturity].

Now thanks be to God, Who always causes me to triumph in Christ!

Scripture References

Psalms 119:130
2 Corinthians 1:12,13 AMP
Galatians 2:20
Hebrews 4:12a AMP
2 Corinthians 5:17 AMP
Proverbs 4:20-23 AMP
2 Timothy 1:7b AMP
John 10:10b AMP
Proverbs 3:3,4 AMP
2 Corinthians 3:5b-6a AMP
Philippians 3:13b
Psalm 1:2,3 AMP
Colossians 1:12, 13 AMP
2 Corinthians 2:14

PRAYER FOR STRATEGY

Father, in the name of Jesus, I offer up thanksgiving with a spirit of gratitude and willingly acknowledge you in all that I say and do, as you give my life purpose.

I understand without a shadow of doubt that prayer is simply the voice of faith and that you are able to do exceeding abundantly above all that we ask or think according to the power that works in us.

Therefore, I pray that as you reveal the big picture to me that I find myself attentive and responsible for handling the smallest details, as I was born empowered to impact!

I pray that you charge my faith to walk out of the realm of failure into the arena of good success.

Father, I pray a selfless prayer of faith that you have equipped me with gifts, talents, skills, and abilities to resolve conflict, create conditions, and change culture because I am kingdom-minded.

Today, I decree that as I discipline myself for destiny, that you will establish my going. I recognize that I have dominion to declare victory in every area of my life and those connected to me.

As a result of my faith, success will not leave any room for last place, but it will cause me to triumph.

To the author and finisher of my faith, the great "I Am" who caused me to be, I surrender to your will of success for my life.

Amen.

—William C. Harris

Notes

_____
_____
_____
_____
_____
_____
_____
_____
_____
_____
_____
_____
_____
_____
_____
_____
_____
_____
_____
_____
_____
_____
_____
_____

WILLIAM C. HARRIS

ABOUT
LIFE EMPOWERMENT OUTREACH (LEO) MINISTRIES

Life Empowerment Outreach Ministries is NOT A CHURCH and is NOT A WORSHIP CENTER but simply the answer to the call in knowing that "The Spirit of the Lord is upon me, because he hath anointed me to preach the gospel to the poor; he hath sent me to heal the brokenhearted, to preach deliverance to the captives, and recovering of sight to the blind, to set at liberty them that are bruised, to preach the acceptable year of the Lord" (Luke 4:18-19).

Life Empowerment Outreach Ministries understands the ever-changing times in ministry and is therefore bringing the church right where YOU are! It is our endeavor to empower the common masses with a post-modern and contemporary experience through biblical principles that are foundational to developing a relationship with Jesus Christ. As ministers of the gospel of Jesus Christ we understand that "Our position may be in the pulpit but our place is amongst the people."

Life Empowerment Outreach Ministries is:

RIGOR
We challenge you to work-out in the word...exercise your faith!

RELEVANT
Real Fresh Word! Keeping it one hundred and update that relates to your everyday experiences

RELATIONSHIP
Religion is GOOD, but Relationship is BETTER!

Join LEO Ministries!!!

Life Empowerment Outreach Ministries wants to hear from you. We would like to extend ourselves to you and accepts your comments. Don't stop with reading this book, talk back, interact and join us.

You can find all information about LEO Ministries and listings for upcoming events on our website:

http://www.leoministries.org

And email your comments, thoughts and encouragement to:

info@leoministries.org

We believe that prayer changes things. Those who are in need of prayer, we stand in agreement with you and welcome all prayer request. We have ongoing prayer support for all those who need it (and we all do). Email us with your concerns or the names of those you wish to pray over, and we will bring all of your needs to the Lord.

May God richly bless you lives!

BOOKING SPEAKING ENGAGEMENTS
WITH
ELDER W. CHRIS HARRIS

Elder Harris is Empowered to Impact, living out loud and in relationship with the Lord!

If you are interested in booking Elder Chris Harris for an engagement, please contact LEO Ministries.

We welcome the opportunity to bring the Sports Illustrated Strategies for Success to your next event!

Does your event have a different theme? Elder Harris can craft a targeted message of inspiration and uplifting to bring the Word of God straight to you where you are.

Contact Us:

Email: info@leoministries.org

Website: http://www.leoministries.org

CONTACT THE AUTHOR

I would love to hear from you, so don't be shy, hit me up!

Friend me on Facebook:

* Facebook.com/LEOMinistries

Send me an email:

* info@leoministries.org

Show some love on the websites:

* http://www.leoministries.org
* http://www.brownsfaithtemple.org

Spread the love! And remember, you are already chosen for success, you just have to choose the right path.

STAY TUNED FOR THE NEXT INSTALLMENT

BECAUSE

SUCCESS DOESN'T END HERE

BE BLESSED!